H.O.P.E.

from

Here To Haiti

by

Grant Ryan Nieddu

Forward by Seth Czerepak

DEDICATION

This is first dedicated to my wife, Marissa Nieddu, who has partnered with the mission so smoothly. I would not be moving forward without you.

This is secondly dedicated to Terry and Donna Kruse, as well as Jessie, Natty, and Katrina. Not only did they reach me when I needed it most, but they urged me on.

Finally, this is dedicated to Kenny Ellis, the director of CPI Haiti, for running with me on the adventure in Haiti. I pray for many more years of working with you on this and any other field we find.

TABLE OF CONTENTS

ACKNOWLEDGMENTS

Acknowledgments and Dedications confuse me.

There should instead be a single section that is just listed as "Gratitude", because my gratefulness would extend to dedicating, acknowledging, crowning, inducting, and deifying anyone who has helped me over my many flaws to get one scribble on a page.

Marissa, my wife, endured countless questions:
Does this sound too dramatic? Which design should I use?
What do you think about this or that? Am I being too simplistic? To complex? Questioning too much?
Her patience has been more than I deserve. Her maturity has been far beyond her years. Her love is far beyond what I could have imagined.

Others that immediately come to mind about this individual project helped pushed me to start the project. Seth Czerepak offered a much-needed prodding. Chris Guillebeau deserves much praise as a worthy journey to follow. His work has inspired me much along the way. Steven Pressfield's work haunts me like a powerful, fierce phantom sage, pushing me to finish the work and turn pro.

Forward by Seth Czerepak

UNITED BY A NEED FOR HOPE

"Strength comes not in numbers but in unity and that unity comes not through toleration of our differences but through a celebration of the things which unite us.

"We are united by our human needs; first our physical needs, then our emotional needs, but above all we are united through our need for hope. "

Many of us dream of traveling to developing countries to help the less fortunate. Rarely do we realize that in seeking this opportunity, we're also seeking something for ourselves.

This is because the thing which we're seeking is only felt during what Victor Frankl[1] called "The Existential

1 *Man's Search for Meaning'* by Viktor Frankl. He wrote this epic piece as a legacy of the terrors he experienced as a survivor of the Nazi death camps. The mental challenges he faced caused his heroic journey to understanding purpose.

Vacuum," the time when the busyness of our lives has come to a brief halt and we're confronted with a deep longing, a longing to fulfill the deepest and most persistent of all human needs...

The need for hope.

As you'll soon discover, hope is the one thing which you'll find in greater abundance in places like Haiti than you'll find in wealthier nations like the US. I know, it sounds like a paradox, but as you read this book you'll discover just how true this really is.

The poverty in developing countries is easy to see. It's in the eyes of the starving children, the rubble of the beaten down dwellings, the stench of polluted drinking waters and the barren dust-ridden fields. The poverty in industrialized nations is harder to spot.

It's poverty of hope.

Why is it so hard to believe that we have less hope here than they do in places like Haiti? It's because although hope cannot be bought at any price, we can create the illusion of hope.

We create this illusion by purchasing a new car, a new house, a new set of clothes, a new laptop or mobile device or by merely filling our lives with busyness. We spend so much energy and money on these illusions, that once they wear off, we hardly recognize the need for hope for what it really is.

I believe it's a longing for hope which drove you to pick up this book. As the stewards of this message, it's also *our* hope that this longing will awaken an unshakable desire for you to make a contribution to those in need.

Too often, we believe philanthropy should be 100% self-sacrificing. Too often we believe that if we are in it to receive something for ourselves, that we are in it for the wrong reason. Yet, too often we also walk away from our commitment to help those in need because of burnout, because we lose hope.

Without hope, any plan, policy or leader is destined to fail. With hope all things are possible. Hope is our last and most potent weapon against uncertainty. It's what inspires us to keep going even when we have nothing left. When hope is sparked it ignites courage and with courage we can explode past the boundaries of our present circumstances and towards a more radiant future.

This is one of the most valuable things I ever learned, and I learned it in the midst of my own poverty. You see, I've been broke, making less than $12k a year and buried in $40k of debt with nothing left over to pay my tax bill at the end of the year.

Looking back now, as the owner of three successful companies, I often ask myself what brought me from where I was to where I am now. It always comes back to one answer.

I never lost hope.

As you're reading this, I'm sending a prayer out for you. A prayer that what you read will spark hope within you and that this spark will ignite and explode and awaken a burning passion which will inspire all those around you.

I believe that when this happens, you'll become a light in a very dark place and a source of hope for many people and for many years to come.

-Yours in liberty,

Seth Czerepak
VQ Success
www.vqsuccess.com

BOUNCING FORWARD

An Introduction

"One's destination is never a place, but a new way of seeing things."
- Henry Miller

On a dusty, gravel trail with the sun beating down on my face, crammed into a truck cab that was made for 2 but carried 4, my life changed forever.

My eyes were rambling over the horizon, trying to trace the winding goat paths on dusty green and brown hills in the distance. This was my first trip to Haiti with my mission partner, Kenny. Why he thought that a motor-mouthed kid like me would enjoy it, I am not sure.

But he was right.

On a trip with so many adventures, twists and turns, it would be impossible for someone as enthralled with Indian

Jones-type adventures to not be enchanted with ideas of humanitarian swashbuckling.

As is so often true of things in Haiti, we found ourselves stuck. This particular time we were stuck in the north of Haiti in one of the more remote areas, Jean-Rabel.

"Pa avion." No flight.

"There is no return plane," our translator informed us.

We decided (or, more accurately, the situation forced us to decide) to make the 13-hour drive back to Port-au-Prince. No truck, no resources left, and no energy, we were a bit deflated. Maybe it was just exhaustion, but we were frustrated, slowing to a significant lack in the hopefulness department.

Yet, also in true Haitian fashion, our new-found friends on this little-yet-determined section of island made a way.

Their sense of hope carried us that day.

They found a truck and the money for fuel, and, in an effort to race ahead of the rains that were beginning to fall, we dashed for the borrowed *machin la*[2], loaded up, and bounced our way toward Port-au-Prince.

Out here roads are only "roads" when they aren't gully washers, which is most of the rainy season. After passing through rivers that were as deep as the windshield, down

---

2*Machine la:* auto, vehicle, truck in Haitian Creole.

ravines-turned-roads, pushing the truck in driving rain when necessary and riding the brake just as often, we eventually found ourselves back on the sunny pavement south toward the capital.

Which is where you would have found me as my life was being changed forever.

Whatever Kenny thought I might find in Haiti, I am not sure. However, I know with absolute clarity that I found something now priceless to me.

I found my new direction in life. I gained a new sense of hope.

- o That spark of direction was not just to help Haiti (though it is definitely that).
- o It was not just to do humanitarian development (which is certainly the thing I love doing).
- o It was not just seeing first-time travelers deeply changed on our challenging trips (though these moments will forever be a part of my favorite memories.)

On that first trip I was unable to describe it to myself or those around me, but I knew it was bigger than I was. *I was _hopeful_ about my direction and future.*

And it is only now, almost 4 years later, that I believe I have been able to pick the words that describe what it is we do, what our CPI teams do, though our efforts in Chauffard, Haiti.

My direction in life has become
the business of delivering hope.

A Destiny of Delivering Hope

My dream is to be on the cutting edge of what moves the heart of people from all walks of life. It is the art of seeking out and destroying the root cause of hopelessness and planting seeds of hopefulness. It is the passion to touch the surplus of hope in one person and connecting it to the lack of hope in another.

This is pure mission.
This is humanitarian.
This is philanthropia.

In that bouncy, truck-cab moment, I knew that no matter where I would find myself, no matter where I would be or what I would be putting my hands to, living a life of delivering hopeful significance was my place, my passion, and my ultimate direction.

Haiti and our work there has taught me much about hope. I have had living, gritty examples of those who should by all means be hopeless deliver hope to those who should by all means be hopeful.

Our Haitian friends have shown me how having *Healthy, Happy Relationships* gives them access to the things they need. Those relationships serve as a launch pad for staying *Optimistic in the Face of Opposition*. When one has such an optimism sustained by healthy, happy relationships, they have the mental reserve to *Persist in the Presence of Problems*. The mere act of persisting miraculously brings *Energy, Effort and Enthusiasm* to a person's approach to the things they are facing.

These culminate in a hopeful attitude for success in the situation at hand and life in general.

Being on the field tests our ability to sustain hope and helps us question what it is we really place our hope in. Haiti does this for us and for many of you who have traveled with us.

For us and our transforming travelers, our work in Haiti has been the testing ground where we have more fully developed our firm hold on hope, have learned how to deliver hope, and have returned to the United States with a deep resolve to be purveyors of hope.

Haiti has become a two-way flow of needing, receiving, overfilling, and then sharing hope. This is our work. This is my life of explosive significance.

And I truly believe that whatever goat-path is winding through your life, rough or smooth, paved or gravel, whatever season you are experiencing, winter or spring, living this life is your path, too.

I cannot wait to meet you along the way.

Most Sincerely,

Grant R. Nieddu

Grant & Marissa - The NiedDUO at work in Haiti.

1- HEALTHY, HAPPY RELATIONSHIPS

In case you haven't heard, it's tough to meet basic needs in Haiti.

Power, politics, and a plethora of problems make it difficult to deliver food where it needs to go, capture (*and then filter*) the water that falls but rarely quenches thirst, or supply medicine and equipment that flows into the country but are held at bay by red tape and attempts for pay-offs.

In fact, we originally came to Haiti during a food crisis to bring rice into the northern region. We surprisingly found out that the country can actually grow enough rice to feed the country. When driving the country side, it is hard to miss the vast rice fields. Despite the production, distribution is quite another story, and that story is often a travesty[3].

---

3   Dr. Timothy Swartz has a lot to say about the travesty of the developing world. His book, appropriately titled *'Travesty'* can be found in the Reading List. He

Our friends in Chauffard face the same challenges in that they are VERY aware that the resources they need are available, or at the very least within reach. Yet, they still cannot obtain the things they need because of political games of structural violence by superpowers and local power-players alike[4].

Despite this obvious oppression, our Haitian friends acknowledge that being illiterate and under-educated (as most of them are) will prevent them from changing these situations. So, they simply shrug it off and go about working for their daily survival.

Though they generally are well off compared to other Haitians, what we would consider the daily basics challenge them significantly. Clean water for Odette to give her son, Danielle, enough nutritious food for Naomi and Chester's newborn, or basic medical supplies and treatments that Joel needs for his Hepatitis are difficult to get.

covers some of the most gut-wrenching accounts of non-profit *mis*management. I do not want to turn you off to social work or grow callous to the humanitarian field. I would rather have you feel indignation that drives you to jump forward, move now, and make a difference while keeping your integrity intact.

4Dr. Paul Farmer, the U.N. Deputy Special Envoy to Haiti, has been a servant of hope to Haitians for his entire adult life. He has skin in the game and has made sacrifices that those who talk a revolutionary game are still just thinking about. His book, 'Pathologies of Power', is a first-hand account of the struggles that his Haitian family (he married his Haitian wife many years ago) and staff (of his medical clinic in the central plateau) have fought through to get basic medical care to those in need. I not only recommend this honorary Sparked Citizen's book but anything else he has authored.

"Luxuries" like teachers and education, which it would take to really give them a hand up to make more substantial national changes, are currently a pipe dream (though we are making HUGE strides for education with our Child Sponsorship program in our little corner of the country.[5])

The Haitian Human Network

Despite these overwhelming circumstances, Haitians find a way. That way is usually what I like to call the Haitian Human Network. It is the living, breathing mass of people with such an uncanny knowledge of facts and events about their country that it borders on mystical.

The number of people in Haiti is often the scape goat for Haitians' desperate situation[6], but it is ironically also their solution to the daily needs they have.

When we arrived in Jean-Rabel in the north, and later in Chauffard in the south, we thought that WE were the solution.

5The CPI Child Sponsorship Program provides for education, supplies, and teachers for our free primary school. Most education in Haiti costs significant money. We attempt to provide education for those in Chauffard. The school will be finished in July 2012. Learn about the Child Sponsorship program at_ http://cpihaiti.org/child-sponsoring/ .

6A U.N. press release states that Haitians are "struggling to escape their gringing poverty and *overpopulation.*" [Emphasis mine.] Poverty is general but ascribing "overpopulation" as what Haitians feel they are trying to escape is mistaken. Read the press release. http://www.un.org/News/Press/docs/1997/19970625.GA9268.html under Plenary 7. Admittedly, the Millenium Development Goals and other academic contributions may be altering the focus for humanitarian work away from population control to other more beneficial areas.

WE brought rice.

We had the education to offer.

We gathered and shipped those building materials.

We were the ever-faithful source of their needs...or so we thought.

Let's get real!

Reality Check, Grant: Haitians have been living and making a way of life for as many centuries as America has[7]. We may bring some things there, but it is their relationships that obtain and distribute the necessities and, if they are lucky, some luxuries.

Just thinking about the people we know and work with, it becomes quickly obvious they live in a very relationship-driven, inter-dependent world.

- Mois drives for everyone.
- Wikinson interprets and guides, as well as leads the dance off!
- Joel laughs all the time, works his photography business, and helps in ways few ever see, as we will discuss below.

7In fact, Haitians have been making their own way since January 1st, 1804, when General Dessalines declared Haiti the second republic in the Western Hemisphere, the first independent dominantly Black republic, and, arguably, one of the few successful slave rebellions of all time.
http://www.haiti.org/images/stories/pdf/key_dates.pdf

- Claude preaches, tirelessly making trips to the various villages while working when he can to make ends meet.
- The ladies make the 3-hour round trip to the water source to solve the lack of water for everyone in the village.
- The families share what little food they have at every meal, giving the bigger share to the growing children.
- Carmen makes dolls to sell.
- Madame Oxylien teaches.

They care! They care for one another. Their symbiotic relationships help them go forward and meet most of their basic needs.

It is not *thriving* just yet, but it is certainly more than merely surviving.

And here is the kicker: they are always laughing! They endure their challenges so well. The ladies giggle as they walk up the steaming rock path with a sloshing 5-gallon bucket on their head. The men sing and laugh while harvesting the fields, not noticing the blazing heat on their blackened skin.

A Midnight Laugh

One particular night after a long day of rain and mud and grime and discomfort, the American travelers were trying to rest. It had been a particularly trying day and everyone was in their tents, exhausted. Lifting a hand to even undress was out of the question.

That's when I heard the unmistakable sound of Jonathan and Joel laughing.

You may have met Jonathan before. He lives in the U.S. and not only works in the school system, but he also works diligently for his family and friends living in Haiti. On trips like this one, Jonathan is the main bridge between our two cultures.

Joel, however, few Americans have met. He is in his late 50's. He has most recently taken up photography to provide for himself. He is always smiling and laughing, respected among the community, and a hard worker. He is passionate about our co-laboring for his country and is not afraid to share his joy with a shout or a fist held high in the air accompanied by a toothy open-mouthed smile.

Earlier that afternoon, during Nurse Troyce's examinations, it was discovered that he has contracted Hepatitis. In all likelihood he has a swollen liver and is in constant pain. The reality of this was weighing on me and darkening my already damp mood when I heard his voice, along with Jonathan's voice, laughing in the dark.

I poked my head out of my tent, peered through the darkness and saw them with pick axes and shovels carving a stairway in the mud. They had seen how difficult it was for the Americans to walk the steep inclines so, in the middle of the night, they were creating a stairway.

They were so full of joy, teasing, laughing and enjoying each others company. They had a very healthy, happy relationship.

From Left to Right: Joel, Claude & Jonathan

Preaching to the Choir

That impacted me deeply! At times I thought that their poverty problem was their inability to effectively work well with others.

> "If I could just teach them *'7 Habits of Highly Effective People'* or *'How to Win Friends and Influence People'*, then they would find a way to not be so poor."

Or,

> "Perhaps they are disconnected from each other and suffering from hopelessness."

Who was I kidding?!

These people know how to work together. Our Haitian friends know what it is to serve each other.

I mean, Joel is almost 60-years old, suffering from debilitating pain resulting from a communicable disease...and he is swinging a pickaxe and serving us in the middle of the damp night, laughing and joking with an old friend!

If only I could serve my employees, or my life-coaching clients, or my friends, or my family and loved ones, with half of the happiness Joel does, I would have an endless group of healthy, happy relationships.

And, if *happy, healthy relationships* can help our friends in Haiti survive and enjoy life and experience hope, how much could it do here in the U.S.?

With the changing economic conditions here in America, people are starting to need help in ways they never knew before[8]. Americans are having to rely on one another more than ever. There is a desperate need for hope through *healthy, happy relationships*. And as a result of this new need, "We the People" are starting to realize that our relationships are not as healthy or happy as they could be.

8As an example of collaborating during a down economy, consider carpooling. 14,976,923 million people carpooled to work in 2010 vs. 13,917,000 who carpooled in 2009. Many will cite lower carpooling rates, but these are based on percentage of population, not actual commuters carpooling. Compare 'Carpooling Rates' under American Community Survey in 2009 & 2010 at www.census.gov.

Not only do healthy and happy relationships help to get by economically, it is so much more emotionally rewarding.[9]

Hope can stir you regardless of your economic level, provided that there are healthy, happy relationships standing with you to catch you if you fall.[10]

We experience this in pockets in America, but taking healthy, happy relationships so much deeper would create a new degree of abundance, and would help people feel valued in the process. Hope would begin to stir in those who needed it. And, I believe that sense of hope would seep into the foundations of social circles.

And, in fact, among our own friends here in the U.S., it has begun to do just that.

Healthy Relationships From Haiti To Home

You see, I got a phone call one day from one of our partners who has helped us significantly with our building projects so far, John.

9According to a Gallup poll of 136,000 people in 132 countries, "spending time with friends", "autonomy", and "social support" were listed as key factors to "moment-to-moment happiness." http://knowledge.wharton.upenn.edu/article.cfm?articleid=2675

10Refer to the work of Professor Cassie Moligner, in her abstract on 'The Pursuit of Happiness: Time, Money, and Social Connection', who concluded that people (duh!) want to spend time with people more than make money. http://knowledge.wharton.upenn.edu/papers/download/011911_Mogilner2010Time MoneyandSocialConnection.pdf.

John was on the other end of the phone, enthusiastic as he usually is. He explained to me that one of our American team partners was trying to open a gym locally and needed to get it painted.

"We need to take what we learn about doing the mission in Haiti and apply it here!" he exclaimed.

As I understand it, this friend was experiencing frustrating challenges opening her gym. When the painting team showed up, a new level of hope surged through the place. The gym got painted. Now our friend has a thriving business in the heart of the downtown![11]

It is so awesome to see that those of us that visit a place like Haiti go to deliver something, and then bring back so much more to our lives in the U.S.

For John, myself, and so many others, we often bring back a much bigger understanding of what it means to have *Healthy, Happy Relationships*, and how that brings hope to those in need of it. This is what it means to go to Haiti and bring back hope in the form of *Healthy, Happy Relationships*.

Once healthy and happy relationships are in place, something happens to the way we view the situations we face. There is glimmer, a spark if you will, of optimism, even when faced with opposition.

11If you are ever in the Lakeland, Florida area, check out CrossFit Lake Mirror.

2 - OPTIMISM IN THE FACE OF OPPOSITION

It was a hot, steamy day. The crowd of children were bunched in the crumbling courtyard, silently noting every movement of the peculiar young man who awkwardly approached the impromptu batter box scratched in the dusty earth.

The batter wiped the sweat from his brow. His face was tight with determination. He clenched the plastic bat and, the pitch sailing into the perfect place, cracked the only home run in our makeshift game of baseball. The roar from the crowd was unquenchable.

They cheered and lifted him high in the air, screaming his name; *"Jean-marc! Jean-marc!"*

This laughing, joyous person being carried was an unlikely hero.

He was born with polio and as a result his legs were bowed and distorted. In a country like Haiti, vaccines for the crippling disease are hard to get hold of in the unreached villages.[12] In all likelihood, the polio outbreak that caused Jean-Marc's illness was never discovered.[13]

The hard life of farming in Haiti is a death sentence for most physically-challenged Haitians.

Shawn Macuire of 316BeSalt & Jean-Marc

The trials that he had overcome in his life and the value he added to the community, however, had caused Jean-Marc to more than merely survive. He has thrived in his community. He was certainly carried on the shoulders of *healthy and happy relationships.*

Jean-Marc had already earned the respect of his friends and peers a long time ago. The home-run he had just scored playing whiffle ball was icing on the cake.

Jean-Marc is one of the most intelligent young men in Chauffard. Though he is short in stature, he has significant self-esteem. He has the makings of a politician or, at the very least, a local leader. He is good with his hands and

---

12   As an example, Kew published an abstract in *Science* magazine about a polio outbreak on Hispaniola in 2001. 12 April 2002: Vol. 296 no. 5566 pp. 356-359
13Page 3 of an abstract submitted by Macintyer in 2011 references ignored reports in the early 1990's of polio which could be the source of Jean-Marc's illness.
http://www.haiti.prizm.org/Polio%20Outbreak%20Haiti%20V%200.3.pdf

laughs in a pinch. He is always smiling, except when he is scrunching his face at you in mock disapproval for some goofy, American habit you portray.

The result of polio in Jean-Marc's life could cause you to pity him. His bowed legs are almost useless in the mountainous terrain of his home village. So, Jean-Marc has to be carried almost every where. But his friends and family hardly seem to notice and show no signs of being inconvenienced.

Before the earthquake in 2010, Jean-Marc was attending school in Port-au-Prince. This was a huge step for him. Though his heart and hands were willing, his work in the fields was more frustrated than fruitful. Thus his family and community made sure that he was attending school. Which, of course, he has excelled at. However, when the earthquake hit, his school was destroyed. Though we were unsure of his welfare at first, we knew that his hope of an academic future were crushed.

The Lost Child

Just after the earthquake of 2011, my first concern was whether or not he had been injured. When the earthquake hit, we were worried that his condition would make him susceptible to a variety of troubles. Honestly, I was worried that he didn't make it.

We spent several days hiding our deep concern. Questions were instead directed to the rest of the community and how they fared through the tremors.

When we found out he was alive and well, we were overjoyed! Then, however, the discussions about his life and future began.

What would he do now that his school was destroyed?

Where could he go to work?

What could he do while a new plan for schooling was formed?

How could he overcome this new opposition to his future?

We were glad that he was in Chauffard at least, and knew that we would see him on our next trip. That is where we found him on our trip we took in the summer of 2010.

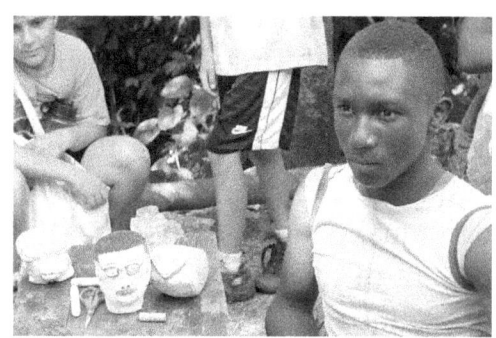

Jean-Marc's early sculptures.

In awe at the surprising strength and optimism of this young man, we found that he had been diligently putting his skilled, strong hands to work. He had begun to work with stones and crafts. His skills were new and his sculptures rudimentary at the start.

But he is smart as a whip and learns fast, and his more recent sculptures showed evidence of significant progress.

You see, Jean-Marc just won't quit.

In fact, more times that not, I marvel that it is his joyful optimism, even more than his iron will-power, which overcomes the opposition in his life. I often wonder if he just sees opportunity everywhere instead of obstacles. He makes it seem easy to overcome these challenges, though I know it is far from that.

And this, I believe is his offering to his community.

An Offering of Optimism

I know that I would have lost hope a long time ago were I in the same situation. I would not be able to laugh and smile and push forward.

Jean-Marc can.
He is a tried and true optimist.

He sees his situation, looks for the opportunity, and, then, like his historic home-run, he gives every muscle and fiber of power he has and commits to the moment.[14]

And this optimism gives him hope.

Though our language barrier prevents me from really knowing, I like to believe that he has begun to get

---

14The Ancient Aztecs referred to this as *'ollin'*. In context, it was a term used in sacrifices when the person commits themselves entirely to the act. It is a divine moment that your previous history has built up to and upon which your future will be determined. All of your energy, focus, strength and complete being are present, and they are precisely executing accurately for the critical, history-altering moment. It is Bruce Willis making that impossible-to-make gunshot which saves the girl. It is Beowulf killing the dragon in a final, critical moment. It is Rosa Parks refusing to stand up. This is the life that Jean-Marc lives moment by moment.

significant hope and joy from the challenge of overcoming his challenges. I believe that every time he accomplishes a new task or dominates a new obstacle, he generates more hope in his heart for himself.

Beyond what he gets out of it, I believe that his optimism and personal successes create ambient hope for his village.

Yes, he might be a student some times, or he may sculpt stone to earn a living. But I believe that Jean-Marc's role in the village is the peddler of Optimism, and thus hope, in Chauffard, Haiti. You can see him patting a melancholy friend on the shoulder, hugging someone, or laughing and teasing. That is his true contribution to this community of wonderful people.

The Optimism Exporter

Jean-Marc's latest creations.

One night, after a steamy day, I saw the community of Haitians slowly gathering under the tarp that covered the courtyard. The yellow light danced as moths flew around it. After a long day of working the fields, the people of Chauffard were gathering simply to be together.

Drifting into thought, I was humbled at the things I learned on the trip. I thought back to my life in America and marveled at how we in the States could ever become pessimistic.

'How does anyone in America fall into a funk if Jean-Marc can stay optimistic here?!' I wondered.

Taking Jean-Marc's example, I thought of all of the great opportunities I had in the U.S. I thought of any of the things that I was upset or hopeless about. I thought of the things that depressed me when I considered that I just may not attain them.

Then, taking Jean-Marc's example further, I imagined the ways I could contribute more, do more, and how I could use those things to be a purveyor of hope, a peddler of optimism, just as he was.

I felt a huge weight lift off of me. I stretched my arms wide and breathed deeply, and took in as much of that easy, night-mountain air as I could. Smiling, I looked up at the thousands of stars you can see in this part of the world.

That is when I heard the tin-can band tuning up. I glanced downhill under the tarp and saw the crowd getting started. The villagers of Chauffard chatted together and began drawing closer to a tight bunch.

Suddenly I heard a metal wash-board being stroked skillfully, with a beautiful rhythm that could only come from a Caribbean island. All cheered with glee, knowing that someone was leading, giving them permission to celebrate, the community rose in joy and laughter.

The older women stopped their conversations and started clapping and dancing. The older men leaned on their canes, turned their attention to the music that tickled the night, pointed and laughed with the entertainment. The children started to dance. All the village was in step, moving in rhythm.

I pressed to the edge of the crowd under the tarp to see the band. To my surprise, I saw Jean-Marc play the washboard.

He had initiated the party that night. Laughing, he urged his friends to pick up their drums and strings and join in. His hands floated across the instrument, leading the entire crowd.

They cheered, laughed, and played, just as they had in the courtyard that afternoon when Jean-Marc had hit the home-run. They were not just enjoying the night. They were in a way, celebrating this young man. They were receiving his gift to them and returning it in kind; it was a night of optimism and hope.

This night of dancing carried hope into the morning empowering this group, as it will with anyone, with the persistence needed to face the problems of the day.

3 - PERSISTENCE IN THE PRESENCE OF PROBLEMS

When Your Plans Get Shaken Up

After the earthquake, our little band of CPI volunteers committed to replacing several of the homes in Chauffard that our Haitian friends had lost. How could the villagers focus on pushing their vision for Chauffard forward if they were sleeping in the rain?

Months passed until we finally raised the support. That summer, an entire crew of dedicated construction workers took weeks to prepare. They finally landed in Haiti excited to completely replace a handful of homes.

Major issue: *None of the supplies had made it out of the port into Chauffard.*

This deflated the team immensely, but we continued to busy ourselves with other projects. There was much more work to do, and one never lacks for ways they can help.

We were happy with that trip in Summer of 2010 when we landed back in the Fort Lauderdale airport. We walked through the business-class crowd proud of where we had just come from. With dust in our hair and a sense of accomplishment in our hearts, we returned home.

However, it weighed heavily on us that we were unable to fulfill our commitment to our Haitian friends. We had already spent the money on the supplies, but they were frustrated with the red tape of the Port-Au-Prince wharf.

Reviewing the trip during our weekly CPI planning meeting, Kenny and I discussed the burden on our hearts.

"What do you think we should do?" I asked Kenny.

Kenny gave me that look of deep, calm resolve which told me that we had no other option but to finish the work! I love an overwhelming challenge!

"Rally a team! We will launch a quick trip. It will only be 3 to 4 days long. The only purpose will be to get those buildings up!", was Kenny's unyielding response.

I probably do not need to tell you that putting together a trip to Haiti takes a ton of resources both in time and money. For us to put it on would be time consuming and difficult. To get all of the supplies and travelers coordinated to be in Chauffard at the same time is not easy. And in terms of making the most of the little time each team has while in Chauffard, it helps to have the supplies already present when they arrive.

But, a promise is a promise, and we were determined to continue the mission of bringing hope to our Haitian friends.

Just a few months later, after another few rounds of fund-raising, surprise donations, strategic planning and innumerable phone calls to Haiti to ensure the supplies would be there, Kenny launched out with a small band of carpenters, contractors, and construction workers. They were like a Special Forces unit of skilled workers with a humanitarian purpose and mission.

If I hadn't mentioned this yet, the trip to Chauffard is a long and laborious one. Though it is truly beautiful and you get a view of the entire central plain; the winding roads, moss-strewn rock slides, lack of any pavement, elevation changes, muddy wooded stretches, and treacherous chasms make this 27 mile drive a 3 hour adventure.

Problems Cause Pause

After a 5-hour drive to Miami, a 2-hour flight to Port-au-Prince, and half-way through that spine-numbing 3-hour ride to Chauffard, the truck stopped. It was a driving rain slapping at the mud, and that changes the road from worse to impassible. The driver had decided that he would not drive the rest of the way for fear of his truck being stuck. The risk of not being able to taxi people in the future or damaging the truck were, to this driver, far worse options than leaving a team of missionaries and supplies right where they stood.

Which is what he did. (See, I told you it was a difficult road! Even many Haitians won't make the trip!)

The road-weary travelers were then forced to unload the supplies into a home of a friend,..of a friend,..who knew their son in school back in the day...*ad infinitum*![15]

The construction team had to trust the homeowner with the supplies and drive the remainder of the road to Chauffard in our battle-worn jeep. This mud-caked, side-dented, piece of machinery was a marvel. Starting out as a brand new, off-the-lot purchase some 10 years ago, the jeep is now barely recognizable. Yet somehow, it just keeps going. (I once saw Mois fix something in the wheel well with a flattened soda can!)

Mois fixing the truck.

The plan was that, after dropping everyone in Chauffard, a single volunteer and the driver would return the same

---

15   This is that living, breathing mass of the Haiti Human Network I was talking about before in the chapter on Healthy Human relationships.

distance, load up the most critical items and make the trip back again.

That's just what they did. Stirring their determination, the construction crew resolved to do the very best they could to prepare the construction site while Kenny set out with the truck to pick up the rest of the supplies.

Kenny's Test of Persistence

Kenny and Mois (our laid-back, yet nimble, driver) bumped slowly through the driving rain back to the middle point where the supplies were. Kenny found out that the most critical supplies were in the back of the room. Patience wore thin. He

Lumber packed into a friend's house.

spent hours as he unpacked the entire room of equipment, loaded the important items into the truck, and repacked the room.

The rain was now driving to the bone as Kenny rode atop the load. The sun was set and the gray day quickly faded to black.

Bounced and bumped and bullied along, Kenny was sore and tired. It was dark. He was soaked. The thrill of adventure had worn off in the moments of exhaustion.

Perhaps if he had a warm shower to look forward to...or maybe if there was a clean place to change from the clammy clothes to clean dry ones...or maybe if running water was available to get the grit out of his skin...or perhaps if a hot cup of coffee were waiting...it may still feel like an adventure.

However, he knew that at this hour, most likely the best he had would be to towel off in bare feet on a dirt floor, where, even though you can change into new clothes, you feel the layer of dirt and grit under what should be otherwise comfortable clothing.

No running water.
No hot shower.
No cup of coffee.
Sleeping with grit and clammy, cold skin was his fate.

Through driving rain and on a truck load of supplies, Kenny accepted these circumstances.

A characteristic about problems like these is that once you think through all the things you desire, realize that they will not become yours, and then attempt to accept that fact; you can finally find some comfort and peace. It sounds like a paradox, but it is true.

For my own sense of comedic timing, I like to think that this is the level of peace of mind where Kenny had come, rolling with the swaying truck, finally accepting the discomfort of his circumstances, and perhaps saying a prayer and connecting in love and appreciation with God. I like to think he was beginning to change his desire to simply being satisfied with curling up on the floor and just getting some rest.

Perhaps he was beginning to be comforted by the thought that just down one hill, over the ravine, and up another hill, and he could sleep at long last...

When out of the black night he heard the rushing water. The truck lurched to a stop with sudden caution.

An Unexpected Phenomenon

For as long as we have been coming to Chauffard, as many teams as we have had there, in every kind of weather we have seen, over the last four years, the ravine just before arriving in Chauffard has never had so much as a trickle of water.

The bone-dry ravine before Chauffard.

During sunny days, it is a bone-white quarry where the local people get any rocks they may need for masonry. You know that when you see the arid ravine that you are close to Chauffard. It is the point where I have developed a sense of "I am home", like recognizing a childhood corner store or a familiar fence post.

For the first time ever, this was not the case.

Along this same ravine, in the black, damp night, beyond the reach of the truck's headlights, dark water rushed by, blocking the road home. I imagine that with a deep sigh and a brush of cool night air that chilled his clammy skin, Kenny climbed down from the truck to conquer this unexpected challenge.

Forced to leap from rock to rock in the dark, scale a hiking path that works you like climbing StairMaster in wet concrete, and sleep on hard ground, Kenny persisted. They left the truck in temporary defeat to retrieve it the next day.

In the morning, another team member, Shawn Maguire (also known as The Water Boy for his work with clean water in Haiti), volunteered to make the trip back to the rest of the equipment.

Kenny and the rest of the construction crew stayed in the village to work with the critical supplies he so diligently fought for the previous day. I imagine that he was exhausted from the day before but lightly refreshed from his sleep.

As the sun grew brighter, his strength returned with the reward of the work of replacing the home of one of our Haitian friends. Hope grew in him along with his strength. With their eye on the hillside road to watch for Shawn's return with the rest of the supplies, the crew worked diligently.

Though no one complained, there was the unspoken concern as to whether or not the crew would be able to accomplish the goal that they had come so far to complete. This being the second team to make the journey to Chauffard to complete it, with all the cost and effort to be there, and the eyes of every partner and friend of CPI in the U.S. watching and waiting to hear news, they knew they just had to return with a good report.

The pressure was immense.

As the day wore on and arms wore out, the team began talking less; quietly yet diligently moving from task to task. Then, immediate supplies began to wane. Knowing that time was running short, the team found themselves waiting in earnest for Shawn's return with the remaining supplies. A pause in the work arose, and the team took a rest.

It was during this break, in the silence of the midday, that they heard voices in the distance talking louder than normal.

There was rustling coming through the damp, green forest.

Though the local families were hard at work, the Americans could hear a loudness in conversations growing closer still. The sounds of people chatting happily, laundry ladies and muddy carrot farmers to then-unseen passer-byes, were getting closer to the American team who slowed to a stall in their work.

Curiosity got the better of the Americans.

They rose, standing to face the direction of the sounds headed their way. Suddenly a young boy broke through the foliage carrying a large piece of ply-wood on his head, balancing it with one hand and laughing as he came.

Surprised, the men gaped.

Kids carried the lumber through the woods to the site.

Instantly another person broke from the woods bearing another much-needed supply. Then another, and another, until there was a steady stream of supplies making their way to the construction site. Loud voices of Haitians talking and laughing filled the courtyard as the pile of supplies grew.

The Haitian peopled had rallied and made the long journey on foot to help deliver the supplies. When the going gets tough, the tough get going, and I assure you that Haitians are tough people! They marched on foot to where the driver had dropped the supplies the day before and made their way back to Chauffard carrying as many of the supplies as they could.

They pushed through the problem and *persisted*, and, even though they had no extra trucks or cars, carried what they could all the way back to their village.

They persisted in the face of problems. Our Haitian friends just keep pressing on!

Kenny and the CPI team wasted no time. With renewed energy they worked diligently and made a dash to raise the house they had come to complete.

Shawn soon arrived with the remaining supplies on the truck. There was no stopping these determined men and women who worked through the day into the evening, and completed the house in the dead of night.

They had just enough time to breakdown their lamps, pack their supplies and make a precipice-risking overnight trek back to Port-au-Prince and make their flight back to the states.

The crack construction finished in the middle of the night.

Persistence on the Cycle of Hope

When this second team set out on the long trip to Chauffard, there was hope and desire to fulfill our commitment and build these homes. We believed that the act of finishing a home for these people would fill them with hope and reassure them of our resolve.

What we found was that the ability to persist is a two-way relationship.

Though we were building hope with each raised board, our team hit a wall of frustration themselves. When you are frustrated, you lose sight of any reason to continue. Persisting in the face of building problems just loses its appeal. *'Why should we persist?!'* the argument develops. *'After all, we most likely won't finish the project anyway.'*

When we quit persisting, pessimism replaces optimism.
But, when we persist in the face of problems, optimism demolishes any resistance.

The Haitians' persistence in the face of problems came through in such a way that filled our team with much-needed hope. They turned the tide of hopelessness back to a rising sense of hope.

Just Keep Going

"Difficult things take a long time, impossible things a little longer." ~ Andrew A. Jackson

When we started our work in Haiti, we were funded at nearly 5-figures a month! That is not a bad start for a non-profit. However, soon after returning from my first trip with Kenny, we were informed that our funding was cut to zero!

We were faced with the decision to either return back to "normal lives", or to persist and find a way to continue. It wasn't a difficult decision really. When we were discussing it during our weekly meeting in the Sunday-school room Kenny's church had lent us, we just looked at each other and knew that we had to persist. We had to keep going.

When there is no apparent momentum, we simply keep going.

We keep making transforming travel trips.

We keep creating events to participate in.

We keep appealing for partners.

We keep bootstrapping for supplies.

We keep reading, studying, discussing and refining our approach.

And...4 years later...

A 20-Year Overnight Success

One of my business mentors who taught me quite a bit always said, *"I am a 20-year overnight success!"*[16]

Everyone would ask him how he had earned so much money in his investments "so quickly."

I could see that he was both flattered and offended by comments like these. He was flattered in that his success was being recognized, but he seemed offended in that he knew and felt the blood, sweat, and tears it took to build his wealth.

I finally think I have a small idea of what he felt.

Building a Dream

Even way back in the beginning, Kenny and I would dream about having a community center. We have put in a lot of work since then. At times we moved closer to that goal, and at other times it felt like we moved further away.

Our first sketches of the community bldg.

After the earthquake in 2010, our focus moved even further from the community center as we put our attention to replacing the homes of our friends in Chauffard instead. It was a tough decision, but what little

---

16   And, I was not the best of students at the time. I was thick-headed and really did not feel I had much to learn. However, 10 years later I am still unearthing lessons I gained from my experience back then.

donations we had gathered for the community center was now being used to complete the homes of Oxylien and Senlis. And, even though we joyfully made that decision because it aligned with CPI's priorities, establishing the Chauffard Community Center seemed a long way off.

But even though we may not know where the miracles come from, we know that if we persist in the face of problems their arrival is certain:

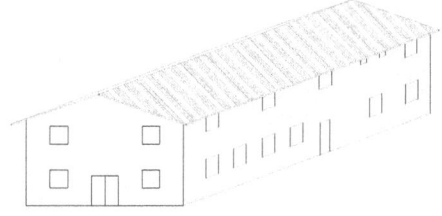

Those sketches became CAD drawings like these from JJ Smith.

"Someone has just written a check for $60,000 to build the first floor of the community center."

Kenny had just delivered a message that took my breath away. We were at our weekly meeting and, as we were wrapping up, he casually started, *"Oh, one more thing..."* (Sometimes, he delivers announcements for their extremely theatrical effect,..and I love it! This was one of those moments.)

We paused, and all of the moments of work, the sacrifices he had made with his family, the low-income jobs I had taken to be able to invest my time with website tweaks and coffee talks about the cause, the support rejections, the local events,...all the "blood, sweat and tears" came rushing to my mind.

Which became illustrated CAD drawings like these, also from JJ.

Someone had actually stepped up and offered to pull together almost 60% of the cost of building The Chauffard Community Center!

I was in shock and, quite honestly, as I am writing this a few weeks after that conversation with Kenny, my pulse still races at the thought.

Many nay-sayers will say about our organization, as I have heard them say about other organizations, *"It would easy for everyone is they got lucky breaks like that, too."*

I want to slap the nay out of nay-sayers sometimes.

Not because they are offending me as much as they are dismissing as 'mere luck' the work we have done to be positioned for such a 'lucky break.'

"Luck is at the intersection of opportunity and preparation." - Seneca, 100 A.D.

I wish that nay-sayers, or anyone for that matter who dismisses the hard work it takes to be prepared for opportunity, could see all the persistent steps it takes to create an infusion of H.O.P.E. as this situation has for the CPI team.

a. The person that stepped up to fund the initial construction came on a Transforming Travel trip.

b. They came on a Transforming Travel trip because of what they heard and experienced about us through their Healthy, Happy Relationships within the CPI team and observing us through the process of the Hope for Haiti 5k.

c. They were able to attend the 5k because the entire CPI team and Lakeland Runners' Club[17] partnered together for the common cause of helping Haiti.

d. There was a bridge to the common cause of helping Haiti because of the effort the CPI team has put in for the last 4 years.

We could track down the intricate strands of the web of persistent actions toward the goal, but I will digress. You get the picture.

The Hope for Haiti 5k to help build the Community Center.

You never know where an opportunity will come from. But, if you have *healthy, happy relationships*, and those healthy relationships help you to become a bit more *optimistic*, and with that optimism you persist just a little

---

17   Louis Irwin and the Lakeland Runners' Club has been a HUGE help setting up our Annual Hope for Haiti 5k Run and Walk. Check them out at http://www.lakelandrunnersclub.com/.

more, you can always be prepared to turn opportunity into your "lucky break" simply by being *persistent in the face of problems*.

And, when the time for action comes, just the act of persistence, will fill you with the much-needed Energy, Effort and Enthusiasm necessary to infuse sustainable hope into your situation.

The Chauffard Community Center on opening day; after 2 years of work.

The first day of school in the community center with Kendal & Zach Anderson of The Crossing Church from Clermont, FL.

4 – ENERGY, EFFORT, AND ENTHUSIASM

What It Takes

Ok, from the outset, I want to disclose that I originally received 'The Three E's' from my dad, George Nieddu[18]. As a kid, he used to tell me, *"Grant, do everything with The Three E's; Energy, Effort and Enthusiasm."* It's funny how those sayings your parents taught you never really leave. (He still signs his emails with "Love...EEE...Dad.")

I have learned that bringing Energy, Effort, and Enthusiasm to situations makes up for most of the gaps in other areas of my life. When I am not entirely sure of a particular solution to a problem, I deliver one or all of The Three E's. I try to tackle everything with as much of the Three E's as I can muster. New relationships, assignments,

---

18   My dad has his own heroic story. Through the ups and downs in his life, he has always persisted and exuded The Three E's. Do me a favor! Holler at him here, http://www.facebook.com/ggnieddu, and let him know that you know about The Three E's.

and personal projects all get launched really well with The Three E's.

Now, I am naturally an Energetic, Enthusiastic person. Being diagnosed A.D.H.D. is testament to that.[19] Yet, though I am usually the only one in group photos fidgeting and generally have trouble being still at all, my level of Energy and Enthusiasm is nothing compared to our Haitian friends.

Haitian Enthusiasm

There is often a gross assumption about people in developing countries. The assumption goes something a little like this:

"Those people are in the situation they are in because:
"They are lazy. "
OR "They don't work."
OR "They are not interested in changing their situation."
(Or pick whatever unhelpful assumption you can imagine here.)

I assure you, the average American would need a whole case of BENGAY after working just half the day a Haitian works in his field. Citizens of developing countries[20] are a lot of things, but lazy isn't one of them!

19In my early teens I was diagnosed A.D.H.D. This crippled me in my sense of identity. I have since learned about the school of thought that channels the pace of thoughts and knows it instead as ideophoria. Check it out here.
20 Actually, "developing" vs. "developed" countries are now outdated terms. Check out Hans Roslings fun and interactive work with statistics that show that we need new terms for these countries.

They face a litany of challenges, and, trust me, it keeps them pretty busy. One of the major challenges they face is having water. Clean water is a fantasy (until recently thanks to Shawn "The Water Boy" Maguire and the rest of the clean-water team.)[21] Generally, our Haitian friends settle for semi-clean water at best.

In Chauffard, they live atop a mountain. It is foggy most mornings, and it rains heavily many times of the year. Despite the presence of this rain and water, there has been no catchment system. The foggy morning rain waters the plants but leaves the villagers themselves parched.

On one hand, you could call the 50-gallon drum positioned strategically under a hole in the muddy tarp a "catchment system", but the maggots and little red worms suctioned to the drum walls makes we want to swig Purell hand sanitizer. For the most part, our Haitian friends do not drink from this,..but *they do if they have to.*

You wouldn't let your family members or friends drink from water like that. We wouldn't either and we committed to help our Haitian friends solve this problem. So catchment and sanitation are definitely issues for our friends in Chauffard.

---

21   We have now installed several units of ceramic micro-filters. Shawn has been all over Port-au-Prince installing numerous water-filter units. The Chauffard Community School now also has a large reservoir being constructed for rain-water capture and treatment. Check him out on YouTube, user: 316besalt.

Exerting Energy

Our friends in Chauffard are not afraid of a little work and they work hard to overcome the lack of clean water.

One of the roles of the women for most of the community is that of water-bearer. They leave the house early in the morning, usually just before 4 a.m in the gray of the morning just before the roosters begin their wake-up call. They walk for almost an hour barefoot over gravel-rocky roads; along goat paths strewn with feces; past the "devil's tree" and the nearby graveyard (ever-so-reverently-quiet![22]); beside head-high fields of yellowed corn; and beyond hidden hovels where the residents chat or laugh.

These are just some of the matrons of Chauffard.

They walk through this beautiful-yet-dry land until the path takes them over a ridge where one can look down and see a lush, green oasis, a stark contrast to their lack of water.

In the valley below is a beautifully constructed arrangement of glistening clear pools of water. A hidden natural spring feeds these pools which grow vast amounts of water chestnuts. Along the

---

22   The Haitian fear of the dead is tangible. With constant stories told about zombification mixed among other daily news, they have a healthy respect for recently departed.

bubbling brook there are a litany of foods and crops growing with several donkeys and cows drinking lazily. This brook rolls on downstream to where the ladies who live in this valley village are washing their clothes. It drifts past the old Catholic Mission-that-became-a-European-Union-project-that-became-a-mostly-abandoned school[23] and continues beyond that.

It is a peaceful beauty that makes me wonder if the atrocities of recent dictatorships and *coup d'etat* ever reached this far into the rural area. But, past history, good or bad, is overwhelmed in this timeless valley of quiet beauty.

Eliciting Effort

It is to this virtual oasis that the women of Chauffard come to fill their 5-gallon buckets. They come, wash themselves, fill their buckets, and, with a final gulp of clean water and a splash of cool refreshment on their face, raise their now splashing full 5-gallon bucket onto their head, and begin the long climb *uphill* back to their families and friends.

Water-bearing is just the start! Next is laundry.

The entire trip to "The Water Source" is downhill. That means they must return clambering uphill balancing a precariously positioned heavy load, being careful not to spill any of the valuable

---

23   This is now a project by my friend, Martin Tierney of Seating Matters.

clean water. They make the return trip over the same loose gravel, thorns, and animal feces they had to pass on the way down; and they do it barefoot with burning thighs and cramping calves. This is the ULTIMATE stair master workout.

Entertaining Enthusiasm

Here is the part where I marvel: They make this journey laughing, teasing one another, making jokes and discussing life!

Typical of the women of the village, this girl laughs while serving.

Usually their laughter upon returning to the village is what wakes the American travelers in the summer (assuming the roosters haven't done their job yet.) I assume the ladies do not complain much as I always see them smiling.

Because of their role as water-bearers and how Energetically and Enthusiastically they tackle the job, as well as of the other jobs they do, the women deliver an aspect of the village that is not always seen by newcomers but is felt in the entire community. It adds a pep in the community's step, despite daunting situations. The spirit of the women carries over into their day, as they cook, clean clothes, prepare meals, and send their children off to the fields, or, in the rare exception, to school.[24]

Many of the transforming travelers over the years have marveled at the women. They quickly see that hard work is not a challenge for our Haitian friends. They also see that, if they as Americans were to have to suddenly be required take the place of the women, they may not have as much joy and hope as the women have.

I like to think that transforming travelers possibly learn what my dad was trying to teach me as a kid.

Energy, Effort and Enthusiasm is so much more than producing good, hard work. It just may be the final key to filling your mind, and therefore the world, with hope.

The Wall of the Willing

At some point in every trip each traveler hits the wall, especially first-timers.

It is not immediately when one first arrives, yet it is not progressive where one can see it coming. You just wake up one day standing with your nose to it.

---

24   This is our current number 1 project; to provide primary education, add adult-education, and as soon as we can hire the teachers, develop a secondary school curriculum. To get a sense of the state of education in Haiti, check out this article by the Voice of the America's news site:
http://www.voanews.com/english/news/americas/Haiti-Struggles-to-Begin-Free-Public-Education-133018688.html

The wall is where you feel like you cannot do a single thing more. You feel miserable. You feel grimy. You cannot think clearly on any particular thing. It is hard to make any decisions.

- Maybe its the fact that you have sipped more soda than water.[25]
- Maybe its the fact that you have not used the bathroom with any kind of light for days.
- Perhaps, its the fact that instead of rinsing off with hot water you have used cold water, then you got sick of cold water so you wiped down with Wet Wipes.
- Or maybe you hadn't cleaned at all.
- Or perhaps its you can't get rid of that rock under your tent or the pebble out of your shoe.
- Or maybe you contracted Haitian Black Tongue.[26]

Whatever the cause may be, you hit the wall.

---

25   With so little clean water available, we had to drink sodas. Even though the attempt is to hydrate, the extensive sugars in the soda cause a person's neurotransmitters to shut down over time. Call it a sugar-crash.

26   Haitian Black Tongue is not a real disease or illness, in case you were worried. It was a practical joke that was played on a transforming traveler in the early years of our work in Haiti. This person had awoken several mornings in a row with a black tongue. Literally! Their tongue was black. No one knew what it was, but the team joked that they better watch out for Haitian Black Tongue. After a few days, everyone agreed it should be looked at by a doctor, all joking aside. The tone switched from silly to serious in seconds as we turned our attention to where in chaotic Port-au-Prince we could find a reliable doctor. At that moment, this traveler, taking it all in with great anxiety, popped yet another antacid tablet in their mouth. Everyone laughed! The antacid tablet the traveler had been taking before bed was turning his tongue black! He had been taking them to deal with a very real illness; travelers' diarrhea. It was a moment of relief, and the myth of Haitian Black Tongue was born!

It makes some want to quit and others want to complain. It has caused one traveler to immediately make the 3-hour drive back to the Port-au-Prince, get on an airplane, and fly back home just a few days in to her trip. It has caused others to sulk.

It is a testing ground. The wall, like a runners' wall, tests our patience, causes us to grow, and, interestingly enough, can make the trip to Haiti profound and life-changing.

The Tipping Point

It can be profound and life-changing because "the wall" in Chauffard, Haiti is the tipping point to attitude change.

When newcomers arrive they often think, though they probably wouldn't admit it, that their actions will revolutionize the village immediately.

"I am going to implement this and do that, and the children will shout for joy, and the elders nod with approval, and there will be much rejoicing!"

Pretty quickly, they get frustrated.

"I don't get it! Why do they do that?! Why don't they [insert expectation here.]?!"

Then, they get exhausted.

"Oh, gosh, when will this mud stop?"

"I can't drink another pineapple soda."

"I just do NOT want to sit my fanny on that dark, dank toilet."

"Climbing that hill does not thrill me right now."

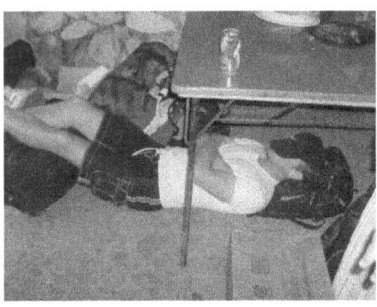

Grant hits "The Wall" full force, under a table, recuperating.

That afternoon, after they eat a stale lunch, not sure if Haitian Happiness[27] is making its way through their stomach, sweating in the pink & blue heat under the tarp, they find themselves laying on an uneven pew/school desk balancing as best as they can.

Stomach gurgling, heat sweat dripping, exhaustion setting in, not wanting to make their way to their tent (*too hot to sleep in*), not wanting to go back in the tiny room (*too crowded*), not ready to face the crowd of shouting children (*too many empty hands and not enough games to play*), they just...stop.

Newcomer, meet The Wall.
The Wall, I believe that you already know the Newcomer.

The wall is a tipping point because in this state Americanism breaks down. Materialism falls away with the desire to just feel relief. Craving the new, hottest movie in the theaters evaporates in the steam coming off the skin.

---

27 Every country has its own version of traveler's diarrhea. Haiti is not exempt! Bring Cipro, people.

When one has gone the route of extreme discomfort like this, the senses heighten; ears get sharp, the nose is astute, and the skin is statically sensitive feeling every movement of the air.

Every sense is searching like a radar for something to hope in. Hope for relief. Hope that the trip will not be miserable the entire time. Hope for rest. Hope for a phantom something. Hope for,..well, hope.

In the complete void of hope is when one is most ready to receive even a mere hint of it. That is when one is ready to hear subtle beauty, to see the world around them and appreciate its nuances, and *'be'*[28] in the moment.

They are ready to finally experience life around them in a whole new way.

It is at this moment, that the sound of the women of the village, the water-bearers and all-around inspiration, laughing and teasing drifts languidly by.

The women of Chauffard working on crafts together.

Hope comes in many forms, but one of the

---

28   Read *'The Attentive Life'* by Leighton Ford. It is very good to help with meditation and being mentally present to help those you are serving better.

most powerful forms of hope is the cool, calm, and loving presence of a lighthearted friend.

The gurgling stomach eases and feels light. A cool afternoon breeze drifts by tingling the sun-scorched skin. The mind eases. A friendly conversation is had, laughter ensues, and strength is restored.

And this level of subtle-yet-powerful relief is delivered by the women of the village. Their demeanor, the way in which they enjoy their challenging lives, makes one believe that things will be all right. The Effort they exert, the Energy they deliver, the Enthusiasm with which they live their lives is a medicine of Hope for those struggling.

Once one decides to operate with The Three E's, as my father was trying to get me to do, our eyes begin to see HOPE instead of hardship.[29] And this hope; culminated from healthy relationships, creating optimism, developing persistence, and pulsating with energy, effort, and enthusiasm; is the building block that Haitians will rebuild their nation.

---

29   Sometimes it is not the situation that needs to change *as much as* our attitudes. Once we change our attitudes, we will be better positioned mentally and emotionally to solve the situations at hand.

5 – IT IS TRULY HUMBLING

A Parting Thought

"Travel is more than the seeing of sights; it is a change that goes on, deep and permanent, in the ideas of living." - Miriam Beardx

Last week we had a meeting with a team that will be traveling to Haiti to meet our friends in Chauffard for the first time.

Sitting to the side with all the thoughts of my day-to-day life conflicting with my yearning to feel the warmth on my cheek and the smells of the fields in Haiti, Kenny Ellis, Director of CPI, brought a cliche statement up again:

When you go on a missions trip, it is really you who are touched and helped as much or more than those you came to touch and help.

He continued, *"It may be cliche, but it is cliche for a reason. It is because it's true."* And I agree.

It is absolutely true to the core that no matter how much I believe we are bringing hope to Joel, and Chester and Naome, and Daphny, and Jean-Marc; I know that *they are bringing us so much more*.

We set out on each trip getting caught up in the conversations of what we will be doing there, or what we will be trying to accomplish, build or teach. We discuss the fact that we want to bring our Haitian friends hope and encouragement.

Some profound moment on each trip turns the tables within each traveler and flips these thoughts upside down. It is then that we look to these wonderful Haitians for hope, encouragement, and a model on how to be so full of warmth and joy in their world.

I long for them to know it too.

As culture and language barriers dwindle and language and communication have warmed over the years, we may have been able to express it in small ways. Our goal is to express it in bigger and bigger ways; to express our appreciation of who they are as unique, interesting, and awesome individuals.

Starting from merely delivering food 4 years ago, to building vision for a healed nation, to creating a dynamically healthy community, to launching educated leaders; there is a two-way street of Hope. Sometimes I simply want to be there to express appreciation for their circumstances and all they have given me by allowing me to be there.

My Own Struggle to Hope

You see I have known what it means to be completely out of hope. I deliberated quite a bit whether or not to share this. Love for my father and mother have caused me to use caution in sharing my own story andw

But I would be remiss to not confess to you now that I have lived in complete hopelessness. For some time, I was determined to commit suicide. Simply put, I had run out of hope.

Hopelessness is not frustration. It is not temporary setbacks. Hopelessness means more than the fact that things are bad. Hopelessness is when you truly believe that things are never going to get any better, no one cares, and no one is coming to help.

I have felt that. The only logical solution, the better option, was death. Being alive with no hope that anyone cares and no one is coming is worse than death.

However, I had a series of people who came into my life and gave me hope. They offered me healthy, happy relationships. From there, I reconnected with my sense of optimism about the opposition I was facing in life. That optimism helped me to persist. And in persistence, I was free to experience the energy, effort and enthusiasm of life once again.

Hope helped me feel alive. And I want you to know that feeling, too.

I want you to receive hope today so that you can be hope for someone tomorrow.

If you have not been on a CPI trip yet, I strongly encourage you to. If you have traveled with us before, but simply need to be moved and warmed again in a profound way, I strongly encourage you to join us again.

Find us. Call us. Email us. Smoke-signal us. Tell us that you want to be transformed and be partners with us, if only for the length of a Transforming Travel trip.

Learn what it means to deliver hope.
Learn what it means to receive hope.
Learn what we mean when we say "H.O.P.E. from Here to Haiti."

I look forward to sharing this amazing journey with you. I hope to see you soon, on a bumpy, dusty road, gazing over this beautiful land, having your cheek warmed in that Caribbean sun and being forever changed in your heart.

Most Gratefully,

Grant

6 – READING LIST

To Develop a Heart of Hope

Though this book is about how we have learned to have a heart of hope during our time on the field in Haiti, it is also my desire that your journey for hope spans far and wide.

I have no doubt that in being involved in serving others you will find hope for yourself. Also consider growing your heart of hope through self-study. Remember, leaders are readers. BAM!

Below are books and resources that have caused me much hope and I return to them often. Most of them are on developing the thought life, as I feel that this is one of the most important fields to work in for the benefit of others.

For Hope

- *'Think and Grow Rich'* by Napoleon Hill

- *'7 Habits of Highly Effective People'* by Stephen Covey

- *'The Power of One'* by Bryce Courtenay

- *'Life Before Death'* by Lawrence Meredith

- *'14,000 Things to Be Happy About'* by Barbara Ann Kipfer

- *'The Alchemist'* by Paulo Coelho

- *'The Attentive Life'* by Leighton Ford

- *'Man's Search for Meaning'* by Viktor Frankl

- *'The Power of Positive Thinking'* by Norman Vincent Peale

- *'The Freedom of Simplicity'* by Richard Foster

For Missions

- *'The 8th Habit'* by Stephen Covey

- *'Mountains Beyond Mountains'* by Tracy Kidder

- *'The Sociological Imagination'* by C. Wright Skills

- *'Bushido: The Code of the Samurai'* by Inazo Nitobe

- *'The War of Art'* by Stephen Pressfield

- *'The Open Secret'* by Leslee Newbiggin

- *'A Theology of Liberation'* by Gustavo Guitirrez

7 - CPI HAITI

Community Partnerships Int'l 501(c)3

Community Partnerships International (CPI) is helping bring hope to people in Haiti and, through the act of bringing hope, helping people import hope into their day-to-day lives in the developed world.

Kenny Ellis, Executive Director of CPI Haiti, and his wife, Jennie

Kenny and Jennie have been married 18 years and have four boys. They reside in Lakeland, FL. Kenny graduated from Southeastern University in 1996 with a BA in Pastoral

Kenny & Jennie Ellis on site in Chauffard, Haiti.

Leadership. He is currently pursuing his MA from Reformed Theological Seminary in Orlando, FL. Kenny served as Pastor to Families with Youth at local churches in Lakeland before planting a church in 1999. He led there over 8 years.

He and Jennie now serve at First Presbyterian Church in Lakeland, FL as associate pastors.

Jonathan and Louna Capre – Pierre Angular Ministre

Jonathan and Louna live the life of ministry. They spearhead a ministry that spans all sides of Haiti. Over 40 years ago, Jonathan's father began to plant churches throughout Haiti. Jonathan grew up in his father's ministry and, after almost a decade of educating abroad, returned his focus to the needs in his home country.

They not only work full time and take care of their two young boys. They also help make CPI possible. Jonathan and his powerful team of Haitian ministers make arrangements, organize vehicles, translate for travelers, and help with the ins and outs of making our work in Haiti happen.

8 – ADDITIONAL RESOURCES

Spark Your Own Life of Philanthropia

Check out these other resources to spark your vision, ignite your successes, and explode your significance. It is our goal to effect more than just the mission field.

More than that, we desire that our life and the fruit of it activates and equips you to live your own life of mission, helping make the world better for those who need it most.

This is our personal vision. We look forward to working with you on it!

The 7-Day Spark Homework
(Free Download)

Become aware of your vision and values. Easy decisions are, well, easy to make. Tough decisions are difficult to make because we usually are not aware of our criteria on how to make the decision. Vision and values are the very criteria we need to determine the decisions we make.

As a life coach, I found that quite often my clients wanted to make decisions that would lead them to the mission field. When they weren't sure of their own values they became stuck. The same situation happens with missionaries.

So, we developed *'The 7-Day Spark Homework'* to help them shake loose the values and vision that already existed.

Get it **free** here: http://grantnieddu.com/writer/

The Top 100 Dream Igniter

This is a tool we spent many hours creating. In fact, it has been through two different brands and evolved over the past few years. Do not let yourself be fooled by the design; this is a power-packed document.

This powerful document walks a person through the process that I have done live for countless others. *'The Top 100 Dream Igniter'* helps you get the clarity you need to start taking action TODAY toward your vision.

To get a jump start *right now* on your own life of mission do the following homework as soon as you possible can.

Can you see where I am going with this? I did this exercise on the eve of my 29th birthday. I knew that I did not want to enter my 30's without knowing the direction of my life. It took me a year to determine my values and vision, align the activities in my life to the vision, and get momentum toward it.

By the time I had turned 30, I had changed from a directionless 20-something to an empowered missionary. I had taken over a branch of a Fortune 500 company. I had written the manuscript to a book, traveled to Haiti over 5 times after collaborating on CPI Haiti.org, and launched my life-coaching business.

More than all of that, I felt sparked! I was lit inside by a deep passion for a vision that had been brewing in me for years.

Principles In the Raw

Many moons ago, Grant and his awesome partner, Jason Northington[30] wrote a series of manuscripts. The goal was to create a very small, very raw series of books that taught just the principles.

People live busy lives. They don't need another 300 page book of platitudes. They need raw principles.

Then life got busy. Well, for Grant and Jason that is.

---

30 Check out the Architect of WOW!, Jason Northington, here: http://architectofwow.blogspot.com/

They were able to finish the first book. *'Prinicples in the Raw: Be – GET!'* was the raw book about the principle of "being" before "getting.

Get it here: www.GrantNieddu.com/writer

Vision Master-Mind Session

Grant has helped numerous people get clarity, create vision, and move toward the life they desire to live.

We recommend working with Grant on a visioning session, or even visiting for a weekend intensive with Grant and Marissa to hammer our your vision. To do so, contact them at grant.nieddu@gmail.com.

In preparation, Grant asks that you have at least accomplished *'The 7-Day Spark Homework'* prior to seeking coaching. It is available for free listed above.

The Goal

The goal is to live a life with sparked vision, igniting successes along the way so you explode your significance by helping others.

Use these tools. If you get stuck, let me know.

Remember, stay strong. Stay hopeful.

Spark your vision.
Ignite your success.
Explode your significance.

9 - GRATITUDE

I mentioned in the Acknowledgment section that instead of acknowledgments I wish that there were a section just titled 'Gratitude.' In light of what I just shared above about those who helped me find hope, I felt that a section of Gratitude would be appropriate.

These are just a mere fraction of the people I am grateful for who reached down to where I was at and gave me hope.

Grant's Dad; the man with the Three E's still living them out.

Grant's Mom who exudes a life of persistence.

Grant's brother, Heath; who has been a role model for as long as Grant can remember.

Grant's brother, Clark (right) on his wedding day. Clark's heart has taught Grant much about love and helped Grant when he needed it most.

Terry & Donna Kruse who, in their obedience to their faith, helped save Grant from himself.

The Kruse girls, like sisters to Grant, have always been there. Jessica, Natalie, and Katrina (l to r.)

The Chauffard elders when they decided on a Community Center. Kenny Ellis at the far left has been a friend to Grant for years now. Grant counts Kenny as one of his closest, most-accepting friends.

The Lakeland group, far more than pictured here, have sown into Grant's life so much it would be impossible to recount.

This group of vagabonds was not only a major source of joy and hope in school, but they have become a continuous source of inspiration to Grant.

And so many more than I could list here!

10 – ABOUT THE AUTHOR

It is Grant's vision to:

Spark Vision.
Ignite Successes.
Explode Significance.

The legacy he wishes to leave is best said in his own words.

"I motivate and inspire, activate and equip, this generation, to over-abundantly succeed at all they desire, through writing, training, public speaking, books, and any future media and ideas."

Grant and his wife, Marissa, work in the humanitarian development field on the island of Hispaniola. They seek to help the people of this island live a higher quality of life through sustainable housing, micro-economic opportunities, and development training.

He and his wife have a passion to train humanitarian volunteers, project teams, and organizational staff to expand their support base by developing supporter loyalty and creating a dynamic supporter culture.

Grant also trains entrepreneurs and business organizations to increase their bottom line by expanding their customer base, developing customer loyalty, and raising employee buy-in.

Follow along with their adventures, their writings about humanitarianism and missions, and how to activate your own Sparked Adventures.

www.GrantNieddu.com

Marissa & I are most grateful for our lives together working the mission.